What Folks are Saying about
THE GROUNDINGS EXPERIENCE

The Groundings Experience taught me how to "see" the unexpected spaces and opportunities in everyday life where Jesus is asking me to be His hands and feet. To listen intentionally, act deliberately, and speak as little as possible!

Sally Henry

Groundings is a discipleship experience that has changed the way I interact with the world. It helped to take me from being an observer of what God does in and through people, to an active and aware participant of what God is doing.

Amy Andreasen

This experience challenged me to look and listen to people around me in my everyday life and be a witness to them. I learned how to start conversations with people that I may not have talked to before and to share the love of Jesus Christ.

Ingrid Daniels

Last year when I took *Groundings,* I really had no idea how much it would impact my faith. I was moved by everyone's stories about how the Holy Spirit was using their every day lives, each story as beautiful as the other. *Groundings* has given new meaning in my being a disciple of Christ. This was a once in a lifetime opportunity.

Deborah Maddocks

The Groundings Experience changed me. It has made me more aware of God in every situation and circumstance: in my thoughts, my actions, my words, and my everyday encounters. Now I think about and see every single person as made in His image, His child. I'm aware and always thinking how can I extend God's grace and mercy in everyday ways.

Susie Smith

Groundings brought me back to the roots of following in the way of Jesus. It caused me to be much more aware of living in the present and truly living aware of "the other." I am so thankful for this experience.

Susan Lubushkin

Groundings assignments helped me to pay attention and notice that God is at work everywhere all the time. I have been much more aware of "third-spaces" where God is doing something in a unique place. Sharing the experiences with my small group helped me to see more ways that God is working in and through His people. And, I have learned as much from my *Groundings* "failures" as the times I have "done it right."

Sheryl France-Moran

In *The Groundings Experience,* I was led through five Jesus narratives, each building on the previous lesson, and I came to a new understanding of how God is working in everyday situations that we all experience. The questions are thought-provoking and the sharing of experiences in small groups deepened my discipleship experience. *Groundings* is an outstanding experience in learning just how much God is active in everyday life and invites us to participate in what He is doing.

Craig Harberts

Groundings was a welcome surprise for me. Thinking it might be yet another Bible study, I quickly realized how mistaken I was. During the six sessions I learned to be much more aware of daily opportunities to be a disciple—to live out the love of Christ and to give and receive blessings to and from those around me. I have even agreed to co-lead an experience this coming year. Quite a step in faith for me!

Paul Miller

I've always thought of discipleship as the application of personal will to master practices that would deepen or enhance my relationship with the Lord, and to be honest, this approach did not get me very far. Instead, the *Groundings* small group Bible studies about how Jesus encountered people, and the accountability and relationships of this experience opened my heart and mind to consider fulfilling the role that I was redeemed for—to follow Christ into the world and continue the work that He started. As a result of my *Groundings Experience*, the question that is consistently running through my mind whether I am at work, or at home, or in the public square is, "Lord, what are you doing here and now? Please help me to be your messenger, show your love, and give you glory." This awareness has made a huge difference in my life.

Jon Moran

THE

GROUNDINGS

EXPERIENCE

THE
GROUNDINGS
EXPERIENCE
PARTICIPANTS GUIDE

Candie Blankman

BVB

Bold Vision Books
PO Box 2011
Friendswood, Texas 7749

DEDICATION

This discipleship experience is dedicated to the brave souls with a holy discontent who took the leap and dove into *The Groundings Experience* wholeheartedly. My prayer is that *Groundings* would grow person-by-person, experience-by-experience, church-by-church until all things are reconciled to God in Christ and heaven and earth are made one.

TABLE OF CONTENTS

WHY GROUNDINGS?

This curriculum was developed to help anyone who desires to follow Christ (be a disciple) more faithfully. It is designed to help Christians encounter Jesus alive in the stories and teaching of the New Testament and to discover where each of us are found in those stories and teachings. The material was birthed out of everyday congregational life where it is common for us to take classes on discipleship and to have a great deal of knowledge *about* the Bible and Jesus. And yet, it seems uncommon for us to be actively engaged in living out and sharing our experience of Jesus in every day places and every day ways—like Jesus did!

Groundings is about being grounded in the living Christ by knowing our own faith stories, noticing God at work in ourselves and others, and opening ourselves up to being part of what God is doing in and around and through us every day.

In *Groundings,* we like to say that Christ is present and powerfully at work in every square inch of the universe writing the Kingdom story. The only difference is whether we notice it and whether or not we offer our story to be a part of the bigger story of God's Kingdom work in the world.

Consequently, *Groundings* is designed as an experience to be lived not a class to take. It will challenge all who engage the material to make discipleship an everyday moment by moment experience. And it will challenge all who participate to make discipleship and evangelism a seamless garment. Living in and proclaiming Christ are the same exercise. As we open ourselves to studying the Scripture to encounter the living Christ and to see ourselves in relation to Him, we are opened to the power of experiencing Christ and allowing others to see and hear that experience. But we are also humbled to see and hear Christ at work in others—at times in people and places where we might least expect it. This is the transformation of a worldview and *Groundings* is designed to help facilitate this transformation.

How?
Six Gatherings

This material is designed to be experienced in six sessions or gatherings. The first five sessions require two hours each followed by *at least* two weeks in between each session to observe the groundings principles in life and to complete the assignments. This time allows participants to live out the experience. Then participants return to the next session to report and share their discoveries of Christ at work in and around them and their responses to those experiences.

The final session is longer, three to five hours, and is designed as a mini retreat where participants explore and discern how they might pass this experience on to others.

Groundings can be done with a large group that is broken up into smaller groups of 4-6 during the gatherings. It can be experienced in one small group of 4-8, or in dyads or triads. In any case it requires a person to facilitate who has already completed the experience. But as we have now learned from two years of *Groundings*, every time someone facilitates this experience, they continue to encounter the living Christ and become a participant every bit as much as a facilitator.

Experiencing the living Christ

always transforms a person.

GROUNDINGS OVERVIEW

OVERVIEW

Seven main components (*) make up the *Groundings* Experience

*Lectio Divina: (May be done one step each week or all steps every week depending on how much experience the group has had with lectio divina.) See Appendix I for definitions and instructions.

> Session 1 – Silence/Read/Listen
> Session 2 – Reflect
> Session 3 – Respond
> Session 4 – Contemplate
> Session 5 – Resolve
> Session 6 – Putting them all together

*Modules: Session 1 through Session 6

> Session 1: Proclaiming the Kingdom – Mary Annoints Jesus
> (Matthew 26 and Luke 7)
> Session 2: Noticing God at Work – The Woman at the Well
> (John 4)
> Session 3: Listening to our Neighbors – The Good Samaritan
> (Luke 10)
> Session 4: Giving and Receiving Hospitality - Zacchaeus
> (Luke 19)

Session 5: Understanding the Mission of God – Nicodemus
(John 3)
Session 6: Groundings: What's Next? (a "mini-retreat")

*Prayer:
For and with each other
For the people we will encounter

*Encountering Jesus in the Scripture.

*Small and Large Group Work:
- Looking at Scripture with new and fresh lenses and open hearts

- Learning to ask questions about the text and discovering yourself in the story

- Learning to focus when we listen and when we speak

- Inviting others to speak

- Learning to ask good questions that invite others to open up

*Journaling:
Writing and drawing and cutting and pasting as often as possible about the *Groundings Experience* during and between the six gatherings

*Assignments Together and Alone
- Taking risks by engaging with people in our everyday contexts who are new to us or new to having conversations with us about faith and God at work in the world and recording as much as possible (journaling)

- Asking questions more than giving answers, listening more than talking being transparent about successes and failures in living out this experience when we report back to the *Groundings* group.

A Covenant for Participants

Together in *Groundings*, through prayer, Bible study, and discussion

I will take Jesus at His word and put those words into action at home, work, school, and play.

I will learn new ways, affirm some old ways, and undo unhelpful ways of following Jesus by taking a fresh look at His teaching and His life. With God's help.

I will covenant to be transparent and vulnerable in honestly doing my assignments and sharing my daily experiences of following Jesus into the world, for the sake of the world, and for the sake of my Christian community.

I will pray for the group.

I will help others in my *Groundings Experience* and allow them to help me in discerning where and how to teach others how to become grounded in Jesus and offering themselves to work in His Kingdom through *The Groundings Experience*.

Signed   _____

Date   _____

GROUNDINGS

Session 1

PROCLAIMING THE KINGDOM

MATTHEW 26:6-13 LUKE 7:36-50

Turning Event

Share (in pairs or whole table group) in **two minutes** about the event/time in your life when you turned the corner from just believing *about* Jesus to *wanting to follow* Jesus. Then one person from each table (if multiple tables) share (with permission) with the larger group, the one experience of another person that inspired/surprised them.

 **Lectio Divina**

The important distinction of going to the text with a "taking it apart" mentality versus a "the text speaking to me" (taking me apart).

Lectio divina is listening not analyzing.

Lectio divina is a practice that must be cultivated.

Lectio divina does not happen easily or quickly.

Like learning to distinguish bird songs, you must be able to eliminate competing songs and sounds in order to hear a particular song. So, too, we must practice and learn to eliminate all sorts of voices and thoughts in order to learn to hear God speaking through the text.

Lectio divina is all about reading/listening with no agenda. It is about a relationship with the living Christ revealing Himself through the text.

Lectio divina is paying attention to how I feel/what I think hearing this text.

Silence/Read/Listen

Col. 1:15-20 (or other text)

- Identify three different readers.
- Take 30 seconds of silence to prepare, focus, put aside distractions. (Silence or *Silencio)*
- Listen as each reader reads the text slowly.
- Be silent 30 seconds to 1 minute in between each reading.

1. When three readings and silence are complete, share anything that made it hard to listen and hear.

2. What are you thinking about?

3. What distracts you?

4. What is your attitude at this very time toward lectio divina? (Be honest.)

5. Share a word or phrase that stood out, but do not explain why.

INTRODUCTION TO GROUNDINGS

Challenge: Look at these texts and the life and teaching of Jesus with fresh eyes and open hearts, not to simply repeat what we already know or have always thought.

Vision: See how being grounded in Christ in everyday life also opens up our lives to seeing God at work all around us, living the Good News, and sharing it with others in a very comfortable and natural way.

Commitment: Make attendance a priority and doing the assignments with whole heart and mind. Everyone signs the Covenant. (Page 17)

Respect: We share the time we have together so that all participants have equal opportunity to speak. Each participant takes responsibility for their own level of participation.

Journal: Draw or write in a journal the key elements of a particular experience in and out of session for deeper processing and fuller sharing with the group (not attempting to remember or speak extemporaneously). A journal is provided in the *Groundings* Kit.

Lectio: Different people have different levels of experience with lectio divina. Please commit to trying and participating and opening up to what God might want to do in and through you through this way of reading/listening to Scripture.

Confidentiality: *The Groundings Experience* as a whole is fully intended to be shared. You are free to share your own experience with anyone. But the experiences of others we will respect and not repeat any stories or experiences without the express permission of the individual. We are entering holy ground.

Define: We will be using the term "third space." A "third space" is any place where we begin to see and experience as a place where God is present and at work. I.e. Starbucks is normally seen as a coffee place, a work station place, a conversation place, a business meeting place, but as a "third space" it is a place where God is present and working in and through people. Your driveway is usually seen as a place to park your car, kids to play basketball, or to have a yard sale. But as a "third space" it is a place where God can be present in a conversation with a neighbor or family member. It takes practice and focus to see "third spaces."

Read Texts

Proclaiming the Kingdom
Matthew 26:6-13; Luke 7:36-50

[6] Meanwhile, Jesus was in Bethany at the home of Simon, a man who had previously had leprosy. [7] While He was eating, a woman came in with a beautiful alabaster jar of expensive perfume and poured it over His head. [8] The disciples were indignant when they saw this. "What a waste!" they said. [9] "It could have been sold for a high price and the money given to the poor." [10] But Jesus, aware of this, replied, "Why criticize this woman for doing such a good thing to me? [11] You will always have the poor among you, but you will not always have me. [12] She has poured this perfume on me to prepare my body for burial. [13] I tell you the truth, wherever the Good News is preached throughout the world, this woman's deed will be remembered and discussed" (Matthew 26:6-13).

[36] One of the Pharisees asked Jesus to have dinner with him, so Jesus went to his home and sat down to eat. [37] When a certain immoral woman from that city heard he was eating there, she brought a beautiful alabaster jar filled with expensive perfume. [38] Then she knelt behind him at his feet, weeping. Her tears fell on his feet, and she wiped them off with her hair. Then she kept kissing his feet and putting perfume on them. [39] When the Pharisee who had invited him saw this, he said to himself, "If this man were a prophet, he would know what kind of woman is touching him. She's a sinner!" [40] Then Jesus answered his thoughts. "Simon," he said

to the Pharisee, "I have something to say to you." "Go ahead, Teacher," Simon replied. [41] Then Jesus told him this story: "A man loaned money to two people—500 pieces of silver to one and 50 pieces to the other. [42] But neither of them could repay him, so he kindly forgave them both, canceling their debts. Who do you suppose loved him more after that?" [43] Simon answered, "I suppose the one for whom he canceled the larger debt." "That's right," Jesus said. [44] Then he turned to the woman and said to Simon, "Look at this woman kneeling here. When I entered your home, you didn't offer me water to wash the dust from my feet, but she has washed them with her tears and wiped them with her hair. [45] You didn't greet me with a kiss, but from the time I first came in, she has not stopped kissing my feet. [46] You neglected the courtesy of olive oil to anoint my head, but she has anointed my feet with rare perfume. [47] "I tell you, her sins—and they are many—have been forgiven, so she has shown me much love. But a person who is forgiven little shows only little love." [48] Then Jesus said to the woman, "Your sins are forgiven." [49] The men at the table said among themselves, "Who is this man, that He goes around forgiving sins?" [50] And Jesus said to the woman, "Your faith has saved you; go in peace" (Luke 7:36-50).

Group Work

Group(s) read and glean basic facts from texts above, recording a list on butcher paper, white board, or flipchart and in the journals.

Questions About the Facts

1. What is the significance of being invited to dinner at this person's house?

2. Why does the story talk about the woman's sin?

3. What is the response of Simon and the others to the woman doing what she was doing?

4. Why did Jesus turn to the woman but talk to Simon?

5. What is the significance of foot washing, kissing feet, anointing for the host/guest?

Compare and Contrast

Use white board or butcher paper on tables, write the following comparisons and contrasts.

Personal Story	Kingdom Story
A meal for insiders	A meal for outsiders

Prayer

1. What is getting in the way of you seeing beyond your personal salvation to see God's bigger story of kingdom work—what He is doing all around you?

2. How might your personal "space(s)" be a place for others to see God at work?

3. What parts of your story could be told as part of God's BIG STORY?

4. Ask the Spirit of God to reveal to you, ways that you are self-focused instead of kingdom focused.

5. What customs/practices/habits are present in your life/environment that might actually be something God can use to help people to see Jesus more clearly?

6. Like the woman, who might you see only as a sinner that Jesus may want you to see as a person that God loves and is at work in/can use to proclaim the greatness of His grace and Kingdom?

Share Prayer

In pairs tell each other your greatest fear/reservation regarding this experience. Then pray specifically for each other regarding this fear.

Session 1 Assignment

❏ **Pray** that the Lord will show you an opportunity to have a conversation with someone.

❏ **Have a conversation** with one person you do not know very well or at all or at least have never talked to about faith/God.

- If it does not come up naturally simply explain that you are trying to learn more about your personal faith and want to know what other people think and believe.

- Ask if they have ever had any experiences that they would describe as being spiritual and if they would tell you about one.

- Ask what they think it means to be a Christian?

- Ask what or who have they actually seen that reflects an expression of faith?

❏ **Observe** an environment (work, school, home, park, coffee shop) you are regularly in and think about how that space might be a "third space" for God to work.

❏ **Begin a Journal** and record (in word or pictures) your space observations. In your journal draw or find a picture showing your expectations/fears/reservations/hopes of this discipleship experience.

❏ **Review** Lectio Divina. (See Appendix I)

❏ **Read** John 4:1-42, paying attention to parts of the story you might not have noticed before or that you have questions about and write or draw what stands out to you from this passage and be ready to share at the next *Groundings.*

GROUNDINGS

Session 2

NOTICING GOD AT WORK

JOHN 4:1-42

Lectio Divina

Silence/Read/Listen/Reflect
Col. 1:15-20 (or other preselected text) p. 48

Reports

- At each table or in the whole group, share about what was learned from conversations/attempts at conversation.

- Share discovered third spaces. Each person simply names the "space" they were able to see differently and what helped them see it that way. (one minute or less)

Large Group

Process for a few minutes with the whole group the learnings from these two assignments.

Prayer

At each table, pray for specific people and circumstances encountered from the interviews and pray for the spaces identified that the Spirit of God will help us open them up for God's Kingdom purposes.

Read Texts

Noticing God at Work
John 4:1-42

¹ Jesus knew the Pharisees had heard that He was baptizing and making more disciples than John ² (though Jesus himself didn't baptize them—His disciples did). ³ So he left Judea and returned to Galilee.

⁴ He had to go through Samaria on the way. ⁵ Eventually He came to the Samaritan village of Sychar, near the field that Jacob gave to his son Joseph. ⁶ Jacob's well was there; and Jesus, tired from the long walk, sat wearily beside the well about noontime. ⁷ Soon a Samaritan woman came to draw water, and Jesus said to her, "Please give me a drink." ⁸ He was alone at the time because His disciples had gone into the village to buy some food.

⁹ The woman was surprised, for Jews refuse to have anything to do with Samaritans. She said to Jesus, "You are a Jew, and I am a Samaritan woman. Why are You asking me for a drink?" ¹⁰ Jesus replied, "If you only knew the gift God has for you and who you are speaking to, you would ask me, and I would give you living water."

[11] "But sir, you don't have a rope or a bucket," she said, "and this well is very deep. Where would you get this living water? [12] And besides, do you think you're greater than our ancestor Jacob, who gave us this well? How can you offer better water than he and his sons and his animals enjoyed?"

[13] Jesus replied, "Anyone who drinks this water will soon become thirsty again. [14] But those who drink the water I give will never be thirsty again. It becomes a fresh, bubbling spring within them, giving them eternal life." [15] "Please, sir," the woman said, "give me this water! Then I'll never be thirsty again, and I won't have to come here to get water." [16] "Go and get your husband," Jesus told her. [17] "I don't have a husband," the woman replied.

Jesus said, "You're right! You don't have a husband— [18] for you have had five husbands, and you aren't even married to the man you're living with now. You certainly spoke the truth!"

[19] "Sir," the woman said, "you must be a prophet. [20] So tell me, why is it that you Jews insist that Jerusalem is the only place of worship, while we Samaritans claim it is here at Mount Gerizim, where our ancestors worshiped?"

[21] Jesus replied, "Believe me, dear woman, the time is coming when it will no longer matter whether you worship the Father on this mountain or in Jerusalem. [22] You Samaritans know very little about the one you worship, while we Jews know all about Him, for salvation comes through the Jews. [23] But the time is coming—indeed it's here now—when true worshipers will worship the Father in spirit and in truth. The Father is looking for those who will worship Him that way. [24] For God is Spirit, so those who worship Him must worship in spirit and in truth."

[25] The woman said, "I know the Messiah is coming— the one who is called Christ. When He comes, He will

explain everything to us." [26] Then Jesus told her, "I am the Messiah!" [27] Just then His disciples came back. They were shocked to find Him talking to a woman, but none of them had the nerve to ask, "What do you want with her?" or "Why are you talking to her?" [28] The woman left her water jar beside the well and ran back to the village, telling everyone, [29] "Come and see a man who told me everything I ever did! Could He possibly be the Messiah?" [30] So the people came streaming from the village to see Him.

[31] Meanwhile, the disciples were urging Jesus, "Rabbi, eat something."

[32] But Jesus replied, "I have a kind of food you know nothing about." [33] "Did someone bring Him food while we were gone?" the disciples asked each other.

[34] Then Jesus explained: "My nourishment comes from doing the will of God, who sent me, and from finishing His work. [35] You know the saying, 'Four months between planting and harvest. But I say, wake up and look around. The fields are already ripe for harvest. [36] The harvesters are paid good wages, and the fruit they harvest is people brought to eternal life. What joy awaits both the planter and the harvester alike! [37] You know the saying, 'One plants and another harvests.' And it's true. [38] I sent you to harvest where you didn't plant; others had already done the work, and now you will get to gather the harvest."

[39] Many Samaritans from the village believed in Jesus because the woman had said, "He told me everything I ever did!" [40] When they came out to see Him, they begged Him to stay in their village. So He stayed for two days, [41] long enough for many more to hear His message and believe. [42] Then they said to the woman, "Now we believe, not just because of what you told us, but because we have heard Him ourselves. Now we know that He is indeed the Savior of the world" (John 4:1-42 NLT).

In your journal, list the basic facts of the story. Pay attention to the differences between the woman and the disciples.

Group Work

Questions About the Text

1. What is the significance of where Jesus encounters the woman?

2. What does the text say about conversations between Jews and Samaritans and men and women?

3. What does He engage in conversation with her about?

4. What is the evidence of the earthly story?

5. What is the evidence of the Kingdom story?

6. How does Jesus connect them?

7. Why do you think she asks about worship?

8. What is the significance of Jesus' response?

9. What is the woman's response to listening to Jesus? What is the evidence that she believes?

10. What is the connection between Jesus' conversation with the woman and His conversation with the disciples about food?

11. Who in the story was doing Kingdom work?

Compare and Contrast

Experience of Woman	Experience of Disciples
Stops what she is doing to learn	Task oriented—get lunch (all of them?)

Large Group

Work together to rewrite (out loud) the disciples' story so that they are Kingdom focused. Use the following questions to guide you in this exercise.

1. What would the disciples have done if they had seen Jesus as Messiah, the one who knew all about them—like the woman saw Him?

2. What would the disciples have done if they had seen the town where they got lunch as a "third space"?

3. What would the disciples have done if they had seen the well as a "third space?"

4. What would the disciples have done if they had seen God at work in the woman and her purpose in the Kingdom?

Learning to Recognize and Tell Your Story

Do you have a "well story"—a time when you experienced the presence of Christ in an unusual way? Briefly summarize the place, time, and circumstances (2-3 minutes). If more than one table/group do this around tables.

Write several bullet points of your story in your journal.

Prayer

Pray in Pairs
- For the people that you will interview
- For each other's current story of life with Christ
- For this *Groundings Experience*

Session 2 Assignment

Another conversation: Discover someone else's story about their belief/unbelief in God

This conversation is not meant for you to argue, correct, explain, or defend anything. The primary objective is to learn to listen to others and notice God at work in their lives. You will do very little talking. Be curious. Ask questions. Try to understand their experience. See *Groundings Stories*, "God in a Birdbath."

❑ **What to ask:**

(These question prompts are guides *if* you need to get the conversation going. If the person opens up easily, simply listen and follow the conversation.)

Do you believe in God?

> If yes, what is the God that you believe in like, and where do these ideas come from?

> If not, why do you not believe?

> If yes, was there ever a "turning point" in your life when you sensed God's presence more in your daily life?

> If so, how and where?

> If not, what do you think other people are experiencing when they say they have experienced God in their lives? (no judgment).

I am keeping a journal about what I am learning. Do you mind if I take some notes as we talk?

Can you tell me more about that?

What did you mean when you said…....?

Have you ever experienced an extremely spiritual person?

Can you describe more about this person?

I want to learn from other people's experiences. Is there anything else you can tell me about your life story that might help me understand more about how you think God does work in everyday situations? Or why you think God doesn't?

Phrases you can say:
- Wow! That is very interesting.
- I really appreciate you being so honest.
- It sounds like you were/are really…
- I am amazed that…
- Hearing your story helps me understand mine more.
- Thank you for being willing to talk about this with me.
- Let me see if I heard you correctly. You said…

❑   **Your Personal Story/Tmeline**

Identify and write or draw in your journal five key events in your life story—especially those events that, at the time or later in life, you realized these were times when God was working in you and through you.

❑   **Read**

Luke 10:25-37
As you read, pay attention to parts of the story you might not have noticed before or have questions about. Write or draw these in your journal and come to the next class session prepared to share.

GROUNDINGS

Session 3

LISTENING TO OUR NEIGHBORS

LUKE 10:25-37

Lectio Divina

Respond
Colossians 1:15-20 (or other selected text)

Evaluation

What is happening outside and inside of you so far related to the *Groundings* experience? (Your answers are not a report about your assignments; instead describe your feelings and experience.)

1. First—basic results—What have you done?

   ❑ I did not talk to anyone.
   ❑ I talked to my wife/husband.
   ❑ I forgot.

❑ I couldn't think of anyone to talk to.
❑ I talked to a neighbor.
❑ I talked to a stranger at Starbucks.
❑ I was afraid and just did not want to do it.

2. Second—feelings—What have you felt?

❑ Guilt – not doing the assignments
❑ Frustration – this class is not what I expected
❑ Anxious – don't know how to start conversations
❑ Excited – I am learning a lot from talking to others
❑ Embarrassed – I thought I knew more than I do
❑ Amazed – I am seeing God at work a lot more
❑ Confused – don't know what to think, mixed feelings

Reports

With your group, share your discoveries from your personal story/time line and your conversations.

Your time line/story

1. What did you realize about your personal faith story that you had not realized before?

2. What and/or who stood out in your recollection?

3. Was anything missing from your stories?

Your interviews/conversations with others.

1. What surprised you?

2. What made you uncomfortable?

3. Did you ask questions? If so, what kind of questions did you ask?

4. How willing to talk were they? More or less than expected?

Large Group Share

Each group determines the top two discoveries from each experience of writing their story and interviewing another person. Then one person from each table/group shares these with the larger group.

> For example: "We all were surprised at how willing people were to talk" or "Everyone in our group was uncomfortable beginning the conversation."

Pray in Pairs
- For those struggling with the assignments.

Share in Pairs
- Who is a person that helped you to see God at work, and how did they help you?
- Pray, giving thanks for these people.

Read Text

Listening to My Neighbors
Luke 10:25-37

25 One day an expert in religious law stood up to test Jesus by asking Him this question: "Teacher, what should I do to inherit eternal life?" 26 Jesus replied, "What does the law of Moses say? How do you read it?" 27 The man answered, "You must love the Lord your God with all your heart, all your soul, all your strength, and all your mind.' And, 'Love your neighbor as yourself.'" 28 "Right!" Jesus told him. "Do this and you will live!" 29 The man wanted to justify his actions, so he asked Jesus, "And who is my neighbor?"

30 Jesus replied with a story: "A Jewish man was traveling from Jerusalem down to Jericho, and he was attacked by bandits. They stripped him of his clothes,

beat him up, and left him half dead beside the road. [31] By chance a priest came along. But when he saw the man lying there, he crossed to the other side of the road and passed him by. [32] A Temple assistant walked over and looked at him lying there, but he also passed by on the other side. [33] Then a despised Samaritan came along, and when he saw the man, he felt compassion for him. [34] Going over to him, the Samaritan soothed his wounds with olive oil and wine and bandaged them. Then he put the man on his own donkey and took him to an inn, where he took care of him. [35] The next day he handed the innkeeper two silver coins, telling him, 'Take care of this man. If his bill runs higher than this, I'll pay you the next time I'm here.' [36] Now which of these three would you say was a neighbor to the man who was attacked by bandits?" Jesus asked. [37] The man replied, "The one who showed him mercy." [38] Then Jesus said, "Yes, now go and do the same" (Luke 10:25-37 NLT).

Group Work

Questions About the Text

As a group, discuss the text. Record facts and questions in your journal.

Questions About the Facts

1. What made the man an expert in the law?

2. Was the man primarily interested in the answer to his question? What about the text indicates otherwise?

3. Is it important that Jesus asks two questions in response rather than one? What was the difference between the two questions?

4. Was the expert quoting from the law? If so where?

5. What actions was the expert trying to justify?

6. Why do you think Jesus describes the second man as a temple assistant?

7. Who despised the Samaritan man?

8. What was the extent of the Samaritans care?

9. What is indicated about the Samaritan man by the fact that he could leave this sick man at the inn saying he would return and pay any extra cost later?

10. Why is it important that Jesus asks a question after telling the story?

11. Is Jesus' answer a direct answer to the expert's original question or something else?

Questions for Table Discussion

1. Do we ever use "questions" for a reason other than finding an answer?

2. How do we respond to challenges to our faith or convictions?

3. How did the Pharisee's "questions" affect his neighborliness?

4. What are *our* obstacles to neighborliness?

5. Pray for each other to see and respond to their neighbors.

Identify Your Neighbor

1. Discuss how you can discern_who is your neighbor?

2. Talk about who God might be leading you to in order to be a neighbor like the one in the story of the Good Samaritan?

3. Each person identifies at least one person.

4. Table group help brainstorm how each of these persons might be approached.

 **Prayer**

In pairs, pray for each other and the person each of you has identified.

Session 3 Assignment

❑ **Plan a Neighborhood Observation Exercise**

Go out together (in pairs or together to a larger space)
For Questions to ask and things to look for, see **Neighborhood Observation Exercise** in Appendix III

❑ **Identify two places in your space where you encounter "neighbors."**

Take photos of these places to share with the group.

❑ **Try to encounter at least one such neighbor and record the experience.**

In your journal, write or draw about the experience.

❑ **Continue working on your story**

❑ **Read Luke 19:1-10**

GROUNDINGS

Session 4

GIVING AND RECEIVING HOSPITALITY

LUKE 19:1-10

Lectio Divina

Contemplate
Colossians 1:15-20 (or other selected text)

Going-Out-to-Observe Reports

From neighborhood discoveries

1. What did you see and hear in your "neighborhood?" Or the neighborhood you walked?

2. Did you observe or can you imagine any "third spaces" places?

3. What obstacles (mental or physical) did you encounter?

4. What is the most difficult place you entered, the most challenging people to see or approach like the neighborhood/neighbor that Jesus describes?

One neighbor encounter

1. What conversations did you overhear?

2. What conversations did you join? How?

3. Were you able to hear or see God at work in this conversation?

Read Text

Giving and Receiving Hospitality
Luke 19:1-10

[1] Jesus entered Jericho and made His way through the town. [2] There was a man there named Zacchaeus. He was the chief tax collector in the region, and he had become very rich. [3] He tried to get a look at Jesus, but he was too short to see over the crowd. [4] So he ran ahead and climbed a sycamore-fig tree beside the road, for Jesus was going to pass that way. [5] When Jesus came by, He looked up at Zacchaeus and called him by name. "Zacchaeus!" he said. "Quick, come down! I must be a guest in your home today." [6] Zacchaeus quickly climbed down and took Jesus to his house in great excitement and joy. [7] But the people were displeased. "He has gone to be the guest of a notorious sinner," they grumbled. [8] Meanwhile, Zacchaeus stood before the Lord and

said, "I will give half my wealth to the poor, Lord, and if I have cheated people on their taxes, I will give them back four times as much!" [9] Jesus responded, "Salvation has come to this home today, for this man has shown himself to be a true son of Abraham. [10] For the Son of Man came to seek and save those who are lost" (Luke 19:1-10 NLT).

Group Work

Questions About the Text

Identify the basic facts and record them and any questions you have about the story.

Questions about the Facts

1. What is the significance of Jesus passing through and then going to Zacchaeus' house?

2. How do people feel about tax collectors?

3. What is implied by the fact that he was a rich tax collector? Is this informed at all by Zacchaeus' promise in vs. 8? by how the grumblers categorize him?

4. How do you think Zacchaeus felt when Jesus asked to come to his house?

5. How did the other people feel about this?

6. Who is the "host" in this story?

7. What are the "third spaces" in this story?

8. Why do you think Jesus said that salvation had come to this house?

9. What is the significance of Jesus calling Zacchaeus a "son of Abraham?"

10. How does Jesus feel about sinners? What does He do about sinners? (vs. 10)

Definition of hospitality based on Luke 19: ***Welcoming* and *being with and accepting another (others)***

1. What makes people feel welcome?

2. What makes people feel unwelcome?

3. How can we "be with others" in space that is foreign/not ours?

4. How can we communicate acceptance in foreign space?

5. What are ways to make "third space" places hospitable?

Questions for Table Discussion

Discerning

1. What are the obstacles you have to being hospitable?

2. What are the obstacles you have to accepting hospitality?

3. Who are the people you could invite into your space or a third space?

4. Who are the people that you might need to accept hospitality from?

Prayer

The leader will designate someone to start at the table(s) and that person will pray for the person to their right:

- That obstacles will be removed
- That space (theirs or third spaces) will open up
- That they will see at least one person to invite
- That they will be open to at least one invitation of others

Session 4 Assignment

❑ **Invite someone(s) into your space and record the experiment in your journal.**

How did you identify the person(s)?

How did it feel to invite them?

How did they respond?

What was the best part and worst part of the experience?

❑ **Accept an invitation into someone else's space and record the experience in your journal.**

How did you recognize the invitation?

How did it feel to accept it?

How did you respond

What was the best and worst part of the whole experience?

❑ **Finish your story or time line. Come to the next gathering prepared to share parts of your story with your small group.**

❑ **Read John 3:1-10, 14-17. Record new insights and questions in your journal.**

GROUNDINGS

Session 5

UNDERSTANDING THE MISSION OF GOD

JOHN 3: 1-10, 14-17

Evaluation

Overall feedback.

1. What progress have you personally made from these *Groundings* experiences?

2. In approaching the Scripture more open minded/hearted?

3. In listening?

4. In noticing God at work in and around you?

5. In seeing and using "third spaces"?

6. In telling your own story?

7. What do you want to experience/do yet before you complete this experience?

Lectio Divina

Resolve
Colossians 1:15-20 (or other text)

Reports

At your table, share about your experience giving and receiving hospitality. Share at least one "aha" moment with the large group.

In your group, pray for people and circumstances described in reports.

Read Text

Understanding the Mission of God
John 3:1-10, 14-17

[1] There was a man named Nicodemus, a Jewish religious leader who was a Pharisee. [2] After dark one evening, he came to speak with Jesus. "Rabbi," he said, "we all know that God has sent You to teach us. Your miraculous signs are evidence that God is with You." [3] Jesus replied, "I tell you the truth, unless you are born again, you cannot see the Kingdom of God." [4] "What do you mean?" exclaimed Nicodemus. "How can an

old man go back into his mother's womb and be born again?" [5] Jesus replied, "I assure you, no one can enter the Kingdom of God without being born of water and the Spirit. [6] Humans can reproduce only human life, but the Holy Spirit gives birth to spiritual life. [7] So don't be surprised when I say, 'You must be born again.' [8] The wind blows wherever it wants. Just as you can hear the wind but can't tell where it comes from or where it is going, so you can't explain how people are born of the Spirit." [9] "How are these things possible?" Nicodemus asked. [10] Jesus replied, "You are a respected Jewish teacher, and yet you don't understand these things?

[14] And as Moses lifted up the bronze snake on a pole in the wilderness, so the Son of Man must be lifted up, [15] so that everyone who believes in him will have eternal life. [16] "For this is how God loved the world: He gave His one and only Son, so that everyone who believes in Him will not perish but have eternal life. [17] God sent His Son into the world not to judge the world, but to save the world through Him (John 3:1-10; 14-17 NLT).

Group Work

Questions About the Text

Identify the basic facts and record them and any questions you have about the story.

Questions about the Facts

1. Why do you think Nicodemus came at night?

2. What did Nicodemus know about Jesus?

3. What did he not know? (What did Jesus have to tell Him?)

4. How does Jesus address Nicodemus?

5. What does Jesus know about him?

6. What is the evidence that Nicodemus is thinking in earthly/physical terms?

7. What is the evidence that Jesus is speaking in physical and spiritual terms?

8. How is being born of the Spirit like the wind?

9. What does Jesus communicate about salvation (being born again) by using this analogy?

10. How is Nicodemus' story being used by Jesus?

Compare and Contrast

Compare and contrast the obstacles to understanding spiritual things then and now. Some are the same, some are different. List as many as you can think of.

Then:	Now:
Mosaic Law	Christian culture/Church experience/Rules

Prayer

The leader will designate someone to start at the table(s) and that person will pray for the person to their right.

Group Sharing

What do you want to or need to express or talk about or ask related to your *Groundings* experience?

Session 5 Assignment

❑ **Fasting.**

Each person commits to fasting that is appropriate for them. It can be one meal or one day or one particular food/drink item for an extended period of time or it can be an activity like watching TV or texting. Journal about this experience. Write about how you decided, and what you decided and why. Write about how it felt or impacted your everyday experience. (See Fasting in the Appendix IV.)

❑ **Interview or have a discussion with an unchurched person.**

Ask what they think God is (or is not) doing in the world.
Listen for obstacles that keep them from seeing God.
Listen for clues that help them see.

❑ **Where do you most clearly see God at work in your life right now?**

❑ **Identify (draw or write in your journal) something in your life that needs transformation as a result of understanding God's mission and your part in it.**

What in your life needs to be reoriented?
What priorities need to be rearranged?

❑ **Begin to think about how you might take this _Groundings Experience_ and pass it on.**

Come prepared to talk about it at our final gathering.
a.   Is there a particular person (or two) you have a relationship with that you could approach about doing this with you?
b.   Is there a group you are part of that might be willing to have you lead them through this experience?
c.   What would you need to feel confident in helping someone else or a group go through _Groundings_?

❑ **Plan and delegate the work for a shared meal for the last session**

GROUNDINGS

Session 6

GROUNDINGS: WHAT'S NEXT?

A MINI RETREAT

SHARE A MEAL TOGETHER

Lectio Divina

**From Read to Resolve
Colossians 1:15-20 (or other selected text)**

Reflection on all Five Texts

My favorite text is…

A common theme in all of the texts was …

Something I never saw before was …

I realized more than ever that Jesus …

My other Bible reading has been …

Small Group

1. Share the biggest take-away from various narratives.

2. How have you grown in listening to God/noticing Him at work?

3. How has it affected your discipleship here at SCPC?

   As you go out from this experience?

   In your other main contexts/places?

4. Share the highlights of stories of engagement with others?

5. What was most difficult for you? What was easy for you?

6. What do you need going forward in order to continue to be a follower of Christ who is open to hearing a fresh word from the Scripture, notices God at work in and around you and in others, available to do Kingdom work in Christ's name, and whose worldview is being transformed by the mission of God?

7. What did you learn from your fasting experience?

8. How will this experience affect you from now on?

Large Group

Guided Prayer from the Texts

Pray to become bold and enthusiastic proclaimers of the Kingdom Jesus is building. *(The woman who anointed Jesus at Simon's house)*

Pray to be more aware and notice God at work in unlikely people we encounter. *(The woman at the well)*

Pray for your "neighborhood" and other third spaces that can be a "neighborhood" for the love of Jesus to be proclaimed. *(The Good Samaritan)*

Pray to be a courageous giver and receiver of hospitality. *(Zacchaeus)*

Pray to increasingly know what it means to understand and live out the mission of God as your primary way of life, a reflection of the image of Jesus to the world. *(Nicodemus)*

Groundings Next

First share together in small groups with a member of each group recording the answers to the questions below. Then summarize these answers in the large group.

1. What will the next step be for your own continued discipleship grounding? Practices? What part of Groundings will you continue? What will you not continue?

2. What are the possible venues in your sphere of influence to pass on this experience?

3. What way is God leading you to pass this experience on? Who? Where?

4. Would you be comfortable facilitating this experience by yourself? With another person?

5. What do you need to be confident in facilitating another person or group?

Prayer

- For each other going forward
- For *The Groundings Experience* in your church or area

Session 6 Assignment

Final Assignment to complete in the next 30 days:

☐ In the next week share with at least two different people in a regular conversation what you learned in *Groundings*.

☐ In the next 30 days, continue to pray and determine where/how you will pass on *The Groundings Experience* and let your *Groundings* leader.

☐ Continue being grounded in Christ, paying attention to what God is doing in and through and around you every day.

☐ Continue to read and listen to the Scripture with an open heart and mind with the expectation that you *will* encounter the living and powerful Christ through the Word.

Appendix I

Lectio Divina

"Somehow, I had fallen into a pattern of using the Scriptures as a tool to accomplish utilitarian purposes rather experiencing them primarily as a place of intimacy with God for my own soul's sake."
~Ruth Haley Barton

Groundings and Lectio Divina

There are a variety of configurations for lectio divina. For the purpose of our *Groundings* experience we will be using the following:

Silence – every experience will begin with some time to clear out all the mental clutter and calm the emotional landscape and relax whatever physical demands are present.

Read/Listen – being open to hearing fresh from whatever Scripture is being read out loud. Two or three difference voices will be used to help you do this.

Reflect – to spend time thinking about how whatever stood out to you/spoke to you is connected to your everyday life experience right now.

Respond – this step is not a "what do I do?" but a very open and honest attention to how you are feeling and what you are thinking about what you have heard and reflected on.

Contemplate (Rest) – returning to what you heard and resting in it as from the love of God.

Resolve - this is often where we go to right away when we are approaching a text analytically! But this comes most clearly only after we have spent the time doing the other parts of lectio divina. Sometimes the "resolve" develops more as you continue to "hear" and "reflect" and "respond" to this word throughout the coming days.

Appendix II

Lectio Divina Texts

Colossians 1:15-20

Christ is the visible image of the invisible God.
He existed before anything was created and is supreme over all creation, for through him God created everything in the heavenly realms and on earth.

He made the things we can see and the things we can't see—such as thrones, kingdoms, rulers, and authorities in the unseen world.

Everything was created through him and for him.
He existed before anything else, and He holds all creation together.

Christ is also the head of the church, which is His body. He is the beginning, supreme over all who rise from the dead.

So He is first in everything.

For God in all His fullness was pleased to live in Christ, and through him God reconciled everything to himself. He made peace with everything in heaven and on earth by means of Christ's blood on the cross.

Matthew 16:24-26

Then Jesus told His disciples, "If any want to become my followers, let them deny themselves and take up their cross and follow me.

For those who want to save their life will lose it, and those who lose their life for my sake will find it.

For what will it profit them if they gain the whole world but forfeit their life? Or what will they give in return for their life?"

Psalm 23:1-6

The Lord is my shepherd; I shall not want.
He makes me to lie down in green pastures: he leads me beside still waters; he leads me in the right paths for His name's sake.

Even though I walk through the darkest valley, I fear no evil; for you are with me; your rod and your staff—they comfort me.

You prepare a table before me in the presence of my enemies; you anoint my head with oil; my cup overflows.

Surely goodness and mercy shall follow me all the days of my life, and I shall dwell in the house of the Lord my whole life long.

Philippians 4:8

Finally, beloved, whatever is true, whatever is honorable, whatever is just,whatever is pure, whatever is pleasing, whatever is commendable, if there is any excellence and if there is anything worthy of praise, think about these things.

Keep on doing the things that you have learned and received and heard and seen in me,and the God of peace will be with you.

Appendix III

Neighborhood Observation Exercise

Wondering and Noticing as You Go?

- As you begin, take a quick survey. What do you see that is different in each direction from where you stand?

- As you walk, what do you notice about the entrances to the houses/buildings/stores?

- What does the signage reveal?

- What "feel" does this neighborhood have?

- What are the signs of stability? Transience?

- Is there any open space? Is it being used? How?

- Are there any churches or religious/spiritually focused buildings or businesses? What do they communicate?

- What is the time of day? How many people are out and about? Who are they? Age, gender, ethnicity, etc.? What are they doing? Is there interaction between them?

- Does the area seem to invite people to come out or not? Why?

- Which of these spaces invites *you*? Does not invite *you*? Why or why not?

When you've completed your walk:

- What stood out most about the place you went? Good? Bad?

- What was something you noticed that you had never noticed before?

- Did you see or hear anything that seemed evidence of God's presence?

- Did you see any space that you can imagine could be a place or way for us at SCPC to enter into in order to participate in what God might be doing in that place or could do in that place if we were to offer ourselves?

- Any other observations/feelings/conclusions as a result of your exploring this neighborhood?

Appendix IV

Fasting

Old Testament

Psalm 35:13; 69:10; 109:24—fasting as an **outcry** to God in relation to facing oppressive enemies

New Testament
Matthew 4:1-11

> Then Jesus was led up by the Spirit into the wilderness to be tempted by the devil. He fasted forty days and forty nights, and afterwards he was famished. The tempter came and said to him, "If you are the Son of God, command these stones to become loaves of bread." But he answered, "It is written, 'One does not live by bread alone, but by every word that comes from the mouth of God.' " Then the devil took him to the holy city and placed him on the pinnacle of the temple, saying to him, "If you are the Son of God, throw yourself down; for it is written, 'He will command his angels concerning you,' and 'On their hands they will bear you up, so that you will not dash your foot against a stone.' " Jesus said to him, "Again it is written, 'Do not put the Lord your God to the test.' " Again, the devil took him to a very high mountain and showed him all the kingdoms of the world and their splendor; and he said to him, "All these I will give you, if you will fall down and worship me." Jesus said to him, "Away with you, Satan! for it is written, 'Worship the Lord your God, and serve only him.' " Then the devil left him, and suddenly angels came and waited on him.

Matthew 6:16-18

> "And whenever you fast, do not look dismal, like the hypocrites, for they disfigure their faces so as to show others that they are fasting. Truly I tell you, they have

received their reward. But when you fast, put oil on your head and wash your face, so that your fasting may be seen not by others but by your Father who is in secret; and your Father who sees in secret will reward you.

Matthew 9:14–18

"Why do we and the Pharisees fast often, but your disciples do not fast?" And Jesus said to them, "The wedding guests cannot mourn as long as the bridegroom is with them, can they? The days will come when the bridegroom is taken away from them, and then they will fast. No one sews a piece of unshrunk cloth on an old cloak, for the patch pulls away from the cloak, and a worse tear is made. Neither is new wine put into old wineskins; otherwise, the skins burst, and the wine is spilled, and the skins are destroyed; but new wine is put into fresh wineskins, and so both are preserved."

Luke 2:36–38

There was also a prophet, Anna the daughter of Phanuel, of the tribe of Asher. She was of a great age, having lived with her husband seven years after her marriage, then as a widow to the age of eighty-four. She never left the temple but worshiped there with fasting and prayer night and day. At that moment she came, and began to praise God and to speak about the child to all who were looking for the redemption of Jerusalem.

Luke 18:9–14

He also told this parable to some who trusted in themselves that they were righteous and regarded others with contempt: "Two men went up to the temple to pray, one a Pharisee and the other a tax collector. The Pharisee, standing by himself, was praying thus, 'God, I thank you that I am not like other people: thieves, rogues, adulterers, or even like this tax collector. I fast twice a week; I give a tenth of all my income.' But the tax collector, standing far off, would not even look up to heaven, but was beating his breast and saying, 'God, be merciful to me, a sinner!' I tell you, this man went down to his home justified rather than the other; for all who exalt themselves will be humbled, but all who humble themselves will be exalted."

Acts 13:1–3

Now in the church at Antioch there were prophets and teachers: Barnabas, Simeon who was called Niger, Lucius of Cyrene, Manaen a member of the court of Herod the ruler, and Saul. While they were worshiping the Lord and fasting, the Holy Spirit said, "Set apart for me Barnabas and Saul for the work to which I have called them." Then after fasting and praying they laid their hands on them and sent them off.

Acts 14:21–23

After they had proclaimed the good news to that city and had made many disciples, they returned to Lystra, then on to Iconium and Antioch. There they strengthened the souls of the disciples and encouraged them to continue in the faith, saying, "It is through many persecutions that we must enter the kingdom of God." And after they had appointed elders for them in each church, with prayer and fasting they entrusted them to the Lord in whom they had come to believe.

From the *Dictionary of Jesus and the Gospels*

Fasting in the Gospels

Jesus and His Disciples' Fasting.
When queried about His disciples' practice, Jesus first quotes what is likely a proverbial saying about the inappropriateness of wedding guests fasting while the bridegroom (*see* Bride, Bridegroom) is in their company (cf. *Gos. Thom.* 104) or the wedding festival is in progress. Taking up a common symbol for the age of salvation, a wedding celebration, and identifying himself with the bride groom, though probably not messianically, He explains that fasting will only come into consideration when He is removed from them (Mk 2:19–20).

. . . And He does not prescribe fasting in the future so much as contrast the present fellowship and joy of the age of salvation being initiated with the future sadness associated with His forceful removal from His disciples (cf. especially the reference to "mourning" rather than "fasting" in Mt 9:15, and more generally cf. Jn 16:16–20). The two parables which follow contrast sharply the conduct of Jesus' disciples with that of John's disciples and the Pharisees (Mk 2:21–22).

Jesus and Fasting in General.
Despite the saying of Mark 2:19–20, elsewhere Jesus appears to take for granted that some fasting will continue during His ministry (Mt 6:16–18). In the Sermon on the Mount, He criticizes its ostentatious display. Contrary to the practice of hypocrites, genuine fasting should be conducted toward God alone and disguised toward others by a joyful, even lavish, appearance. Jesus' reference to fasting here should not be interpreted as an injunction to fast. It is more a recognition of its congruity with prayer (Mt 6:5–15) and simplicity (Mt 6:19–34) in the lifestyle of His Jewish disciples.

Jesus' Own Experience of Fasting.
Several times Jesus is described as going without food and drink. He does so during His sojourn in the wilderness (*see* Mountain and Wilderness) prior to His temptations (Mt 4:2 and par.; *see* Temptation of Jesus) when

He rises early to pray in a solitary location (Mk 1:35) and as a result of His ministering to those in need (Mk 8:31). On one occasion He declared to His disciples that He had "food" to eat of which they were ignorant, so referring to His fulfillment of His Father's purpose (Jn 4:31–34). Such passages suggest that for Jesus fasting was often a corollary of other activities to which He gave a high priority—spiritual struggle, prayer and evangelism. He does not take up fasting as a discipline in its own right. There is no evidence that He fasted regularly during the time of His public ministry. His concern that He and His disciples gain sufficient sustenance after extending themselves for other's sake (Mk 2:23) and that people coming to hear him who had missed out on a meal be properly fed (Mk 8:1–13) are also revealing. So too are His associating hospitality with a person's embracing the good news of the kingdom (Lk 19:5–8; *see* Kingdom of God) and with both His and His disciple's anticipation of the quality of life in the kingdom itself (Lk 22:14–18; *see* Table Fellowship).

Fasting in the Early Church.

In line with the secondary place accorded fasting by Jesus, the Apostolic Fathers fail to cite any saying or action of Jesus as a justification of fasting as a religious discipline. Though other references to fasting occur on Jesus' lips (Mk 9:29; Mt 17:21), textual critics are now satisfied that this is due to an early gloss. Such additions also exist outside the gospels and indicate the importance of fasting among some early Christians (Acts 10:30; 1 Cor 7:5). Even so, with the New Testament epistles there is no reference to fasting among Gentile Christians, not even in passages where ascetic practices are mentioned (e.g., Col 2:15–22). However, Jewish Christians, Paul among them, when enduring physical deprivation (e.g., 2 Cor 6:5; 11:27) or engaging in specific prayer (e.g. Acts 13:3; 14:23) seem to have engaged in fasting as it is found in the Old Testament.[1]

Reasons for Fasting from an Article in "Presbyterians Today," by Victor Parachin

1. Like Esther (Esther 4:13-17) – to prepare to meet a challenge

2. To save money from eating out in order to give to a ministry or mission

3. To save time to pray – give up lunch to spend time praying. Can be combined with #2.

4. A reminder that we do not live by bread alone (Mat. 4:4; Deut. 8:3)

5. "An overloaded stomach can interfere with prayer by making us feel sluggish and tired." ~Dr. Hellmut Lutzner.

6. Discipline of our appetites. (#4 reprise)

Reasons for Fasting from *Celebration of Discipline*, by Richard Foster

- To focus and center our attention on God and spiritual things.
- It reveals the things that control us.
- That we do not live by bread alone. (Matthew 4:4)
- Helps us keep balance in life. (1 Corinthians 6:12)
- Discipline brings freedom.

Getting Started for Beginners

❑ Start small. Choose one favorite type of food or drink, or one meal, or one day of the week and limit what you eat on that day. Or it can be a fast from a television program or some other routine that will get your attention by skipping.

❑ Write down what you are fasting from and set a reasonable amount of time to fast. Some examples:

   ❑ Eliminate chocolate from your diet for one month

   ❑ Skip lunch one day a week for two months

   ❑ Eat half your normal portions of all food for one month

   ❑ Limit dessert to one time a week for six weeks

   ❑ Skip news one day a week or a favorite television program for several weeks

❑ Substitute a spiritual "diet" in each of these place. For example, corresponding to the four examples above:

   ❑ Every time you are offered or crave chocolate find a way to take a few minutes to pray or read scripture or journal about your fasting experience

   ❑ During this lunch time mediate on a passage of scripture, journal about what you are experiencing in your spiritual life, begin a prayer journal and use this time to record prayers and any answers, practice lectio and listening

   ❑ Every day you limit your portions set aside some time to read and meditate on scripture, journal about your spiritual experiences, or spend time praying, or practice lectio divina and listening

   ❑ The days you eliminate dessert set aside time to pray, meditate, or journal

   ❑ Use the normal news time or television time to read and meditate on scripture or pray

About the Author

Candie Blankman has been in ministry more than thirty years and an ordained Presbyterian pastor since1996. Candie serves as Pastor of Discipleship, Care, and Engagement at San Clemente Presbyterian Church. Candie has also been a junior and senior high school teacher, a restaurant manager, and has spoken at retreats and conferences for many years. She has been a presenter and coach for SCORRE Speaker Training since 1985. However, Candie's passion is studying the Bible and then teaching and preaching it in a way that reveals the living and powerful Christ.

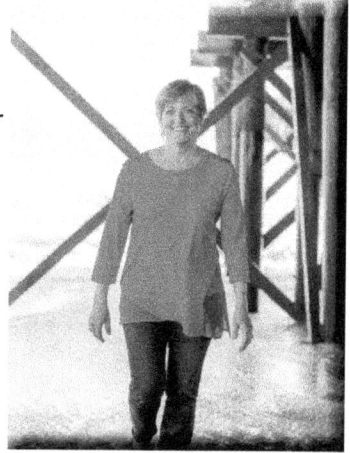

In 2013 Candie began developing Groundings as a foundational discipleship experience designed to transform the often-complacent church culture from one of knowing about Jesus, to one that is following the living Christ into the world. Through five Jesus narratives, Groundings inspires participants to experience discipleship and evangelism as a seamless garment.

When spare time shows up, she walks the beach and writes and paints. She has been married for 42 years to Drew, senior copy editor for InterVarsity Press, and together they have raised three children—this is where she has learned the most about being a minister. Now her five grandchildren are teaching her even more.

Acknowledgments

I am especially thankful to my congregation, San Clemente Presbyterian Church, that provided much of the platform for developing *Groundings.* I am grateful for two pastors and colleagues, Steve Wright and Craig Williams, who sat down with me at the very beginning to brainstorm and flesh out my ideas. I am thankful to the more than one hundred people at San Clemente Presbyterian who entrusted their sacred lives of faith to this experience. I am especially thankful to Sheryl France-Moran, a coworker and beloved friend at San Clemente Presbyterian Church, and one of the first students who enthusiastically embraced and lived out *Groundings* and is now teaching the experience to others. In addition, as Mission Participation Director she has worked with me to incorporate the *Groundings* principles in the orientation and execution of all our mission teams. It has made a difference in the way these teams approach going into the world.

I am thankful for my husband Drew who always provides the space and support for me to pursue whatever it is I believe God is calling me to do. Even if it means being on his own foraging for food in the refrigerator, or my absence for days and weeks at a time, seeing me up late at night, up early in the morning, and sometimes, up all night; he cheers me on with a steady, "Go for it Candie, but pace yourself." I always need both the encouragement and the caution.

Finally, I am thankful to the Lord for all of the grace and patience extended to me on this journey to follow Him and drag others along with me. A poor and very ordinary young girl, I have had the rich privilege of serving Christ in extraordinary places and times in extraordinary ways. And because it has helped me to see the extraordinary work of God in ordinary places, I consider *The Groundings Experience* to be one of the richest privileges of all. To God be the glory.

Endnotes

[1]Joel B. Green, Scot McKnight and I. Howard Marshall, *Dictionary of Jesus and the Gospels* (Downers Grove, Ill.: InterVarsity Press, 1992), 233-34

www.ingramcontent.com/pod-product-compliance
Lightning Source LLC
Chambersburg PA
CBHW080527030426
42337CB00023B/4650